THE NON-PROPHET'S GUIDE TO THE END TIMES WORKBOOK

Written & Illustrated by
TODD HAMPSON

HARVEST HOUSE PUBLISHERS
EUGENE, OREGON

Cover Illustration by Todd Hampson

Cover design by Kyler Dougherty

Published in association with William K. Jensen Literary Agency, 119 Bampton Court, Eugene, Oregon, 97404

The Non-Prophet's Guide™ to the End Times Workbook
Copyright © 2020 by Text by Todd Hampson. Artwork by Todd Hampson
Published by Harvest House Publishers
Eugene, Oregon 97408
www.harvesthousepublishers.com

ISBN 978-0-7369-8025-8 (pbk)
ISBN 978-0-7369-8026-5 (eBook)

Library of Congress Cataloging-in-Publication Data is on file at the Library of Congress, Washington, DC

Printed in the United States of America

20 21 22 23 24 25 26 27 28 / VP-CD / 10 9 8 7 6 5 4 3 2 1

CONTENTS

INTRODUCTION

Living Expectantly

I've never been on an archeological dig, but I'd love to do so if the opportunity ever arose. Long hours in the hot sun, dust in your eyes, digging in the dirt, and carefully removing and cataloging artifacts. Okay, well, some of that doesn't sound so fun, but the excitement of the discovery and prospect of understanding the bigger picture as we put the puzzle pieces together definitely does. Those who pay their dues during long days in the searing heat reap the reward of thrilling new discoveries and a broader understanding. An artifact by itself is mildly interesting, but when integrated into the bigger picture that reveals the ancient culture buried in the strata waiting to be discovered—the results are truly exhilarating.

Metaphorically speaking, this is the case with any in-depth Bible study adventure. We're familiar with our favorite topics, but when we take the time to study them systematically, what we learn becomes truly thrilling. When we endeavor to more thoroughly understand an area of theology, or a specific topic in Scripture, it is akin to roping off an archeological site in preparation for a professional dig. As we grid the landscape, assemble our tools, and plan our work, the excitement builds as we anticipate the exciting new truths we're about to uncover.

You are a rarity. Most people will not take the time to embark upon a dedicated journey into Bible prophecy and eschatology. Many avoid the book of Revelation like the plagues that are detailed in its pages. But you are different. You want to know more. Along your journey you've learned that the more you study Scripture, the more you realize its divine nature. Most importantly, as you study the Word of God, you fall deeper in love with the God of the Word.

Scripture is like a divine roadmap. It is our spiritual GPS, pinpointing where we are on God's prophetic calendar. As we prayerfully study God's prophetic Word, it also gives us personal insight into our calling. God has sovereignly placed us at this time in history when all the signs seem to be pointing to the Lord's soon return, and those of us who know the Savior each have a specific calling at this critical moment.

My prayer is that you would use this workbook in conjunction with *The Non-Prophet's Guide™ to the End Times* so you can form deep and lasting convictions about end-time events. I also pray this study will help you make sense of the world today and discover a little more about your personal calling as you serve God in your generation. We live in a day that many generations of believers have longed to see. The season in which we live has many of the hallmarks of the period just prior to the first coming of Jesus.

The clear timeframe for the first arrival of the Messiah was provided in Daniel chapter 9. This mega-prophecy—along with hundreds of additional prophecies—armed first-century students of Scripture with a clear understanding of the timing for his arrival.

Yet few understood and fewer really believed the prophecies enough to actively watch. Old Simeon and Anna (Luke chapter 2) were among the few—part of the remnant who studied, believed, and worked while they watched and waited.

As you begin this journey, I want to encourage you to follow their example. Study carefully what Scripture teaches about prophecy and the end times. Believe God's Word and take it at face value. Watch the events, conditions, and signs of our day with an eye to the sky in apt anticipation of an otherworldly shout, a cosmic trumpet blast, and a super-natural cumulonimbus cloud formation.

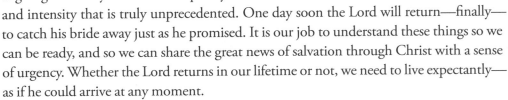

The rapture is even more immi-nent than it was in generations past. I know that statement is redun-dant because *imminent* means "at any moment," but signs and conditions are aligning in our day at a level of frequency and intensity that is truly unprecedented. One day soon the Lord will return—finally—to catch his bride away just as he promised. It is our job to understand these things so we can be ready, and so we can share the great news of salvation through Christ with a sense of urgency. Whether the Lord returns in our lifetime or not, we need to live expectantly—as if he could arrive at any moment.

One last thing I have to mention: If you are reading this and have not yet asked Christ to be your Savior, please do so now. Otherwise this journey will be nothing more than an intellectual pursuit. When you accept Christ, the Holy Spirit comes to indwell you. This means he takes up residence in you and illumines Scripture to you as you read it.

If you have not yet accepted Jesus but would like to do so now, break the rules and skip ahead to chapter 20 of *The Non-Prophet's Guide™ to the End Times* to learn exactly what it means to receive Christ and become a Christian.

LESSON 1

Unique to the Bible

(The Non-Prophet's Guide™ to the End Times, Chapter 1)

Bible prophecy is the central nervous system of the Bible. Every key narrative, theme, person, and line of theology ties back into Bible prophecy. A full one-third of the Bible is prophetic in nature. The first prophecy in Scripture is found in Genesis 3:15. This prophecy, known as the protoevangelium, is the first hint of a future Savior. The preceding two chapters provide the necessary backstory that make Genesis 3:15 so compelling. In Genesis 3, Eden was ruined. In Revelation 22 (the last chapter of the canon of Scripture), Eden is restored and key prophecies about the future are given. So it is safe to say that Bible prophecy plays an all-important role in Scripture from cover to cover. Small details, figures, and stories are linked to the greater meta-narrative of Scripture through the connecting fabric of Bible prophecy.

39 WRITERS 3 CONTINENTS 1500 YEARS 1 STORY

No other religion-founding book contains predictive prophecy or claims to be the very word of God. These attributes are unique to the Bible and add instant credibility to its claim to divine origin.

As we begin this study, it is important to keep those details in mind. There's also one additional aspect of prophecy I want to bring to your attention here that I didn't have room to cover in the book. While prophecy is found throughout Scripture, and figures like David (who wrote many of the prophetic psalms), Elijah and Elisha, and others are rightfully referred to as prophets, there are 17 distinctly prophetic books in the Old Testament known as the Prophets. This section of the Old Testament is broken up into two categories—the major and minor prophets. It is important to note that the terms *major* and *minor* have to do with book size and breadth of prophecy, not prophetic importance.

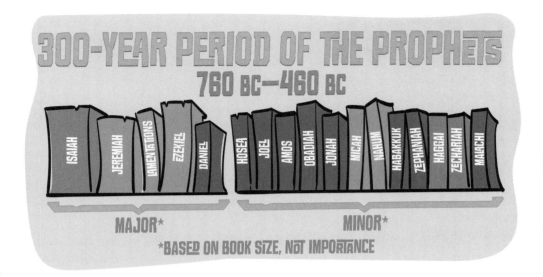

300-YEAR PERIOD OF THE PROPHETS
760 BC—460 BC

ISAIAH · JEREMIAH · LAMENTATIONS · EZEKIEL · DANIEL

HOSEA · JOEL · AMOS · OBADIAH · JONAH · MICAH · NAHUM · HABAKKUK · ZEPHANIAH · HAGGAI · ZECHARIAH · MALACHI

MAJOR* · MINOR*

*BASED ON BOOK SIZE, NOT IMPORTANCE

The books of the major prophets are Isaiah, Jeremiah, Lamentations (most likely written by Jeremiah), Ezekiel, and Daniel. The books of the minor prophets are Hosea, Joel, Amos, Obadiah, Jonah, Micah, Nahum, Habakkuk, Zephaniah, Haggai, Zechariah, and Malachi.

The prophecies in these books relate to the first and second comings of Christ, the tribulation period, the millennial kingdom, and other areas of prophecy. In *The Non-Prophet's Guide™ to the End Times*, I presented the book of Daniel, the Olivet Discourse, and Revelation as the three key books to study so you can get up to speed quickly.

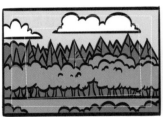  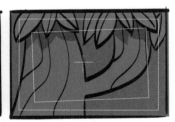

After you have read and studied those sections of Scripture, I would encourage you to study the other great prophetic chapters and books as well. You will be amazed at the details provided and how they fit into the framework you have already studied.

VERSES TO CONSIDER

The essence of prophecy is to give a clear witness for Jesus.

—REVELATION 19:10 (NLT)

> *I will put enmity between you and the woman, and between your offspring and hers; he will crush your head, and you will strike his heel.*
>
> **—GENESIS 3:15**

> *Above all, you must understand that no prophecy of Scripture came about by the prophet's own interpretation of things. For prophecy never had its origin in the human will, but prophets, though human, spoke from God as they were carried along by the Holy Spirit.*
>
> **—2 PETER 1:20-21**

STUDY QUESTIONS

What jumps out at you from the verses above? What hadn't you noticed before?

Did you realize that one-third of the Bible is prophetic in nature?

How does this affect your view of Scripture?

How might this add depth and interest to areas of Scripture once thought of as boring or relatively unimportant?

Does the world seem a scarier place to you now than it was five to ten years ago? Why or why not?

How does a study of Bible prophecy help us make sense of the conditions of the world around us?

How do fulfilled Bible prophecies affect our view of yet-to-be-fulfilled Bible prophecies?

Does the Lord's future return seem distant or irrelevant? Why or why not?

How are you affected by the knowledge that the rapture could happen in your lifetime?

Do you have any reservations about studying Bible prophecy in general, or the end times specifically?

APPLICATION

What will you take away from today's study? How will it influence you from a practical standpoint?

What has the Lord brought to your attention today that affects you on a spiritual and emotional level (more joy, confidence, etc.)? Journal your thoughts below.

What detail about Bible prophecy became clear to you today? Take some time to talk to God about it right now, then journal what you sense he is teaching you.

PRAYER

LORD, help me as I begin this study. I commit this time and energy to you, and I pray that you will guide me into truth. Help me to grow closer to you as a result of taking on this challenge. Reveal your prophetic Word to me and help me to form biblically based convictions that lead me to an accurate view of who you are and how I can serve you better today than I did yesterday. In Jesus's name, amen.

BIBLE PROPHECY AS AN APOLOGETIC

LESSON 2

Bible Prophecy as an Apologetic

(The Non-Prophet's Guide™ to the End Times, Chapter 2)

Depending on how you categorize prophecy, approximately one-third of the Bible is prophetic in nature. More than 10,000 of the 31,102 verses in the Bible contain prophecy, and many of those have already been fulfilled. God has put his money where his mouth is and demonstrated his promise-keeping faithfulness to generations of believers.

When I was in eighth grade I began to seriously consider the claims of the Bible. Initially I saw it as an unreliable book of fairy tales with bits of wisdom. The key point that caused me to reconsider my position was the fact of fulfilled Bible prophecy. Hundreds of verses and thousands of details foretold in Scripture had come to pass. At first, I doubted this fact until I began to check it out for myself. Even at the age of 13, my doubts were real, but so was the unstoppable proof of fulfilled prophecy.

Perhaps you or someone you know is looking for valid evidence that the Bible is from God. I would encourage anyone who wants to test Scripture or to strengthen their faith to study various Old Testament prophecies that have been fulfilled. For example, every Old Testament prophet except Jonah predicted that Israel, after its people had been scattered around the world, would become a nation again. This amazing prophecy was fulfilled in 1948. This and several other major fulfilled prophecies are detailed in chapter 2 of *The Non-Prophet's Guide™ to the End Times*. I would encourage you to get familiar with those prophecies so you can readily share about them when the opportunity arises.

VERSES TO CONSIDER

I am God, and there is none like me. I make known the end from the beginning, from ancient times, what is still to come.

—ISAIAH 46:9-10

> *I am the LORD; that is my name! I will not give my glory to anyone else, nor share my praise with carved idols. Everything I prophesied has come true, and now I will prophesy again. I will tell you the future before it happens.*
>
> **—ISAIAH 42:8-9 [NLT]**

STUDY QUESTIONS

Have you given much thought to the fact that God is timeless, or outside of time? Why is this significant when it comes to Bible prophecy?

What other evidence do you think demonstrates the Bible is from God?

What factors cause people to doubt the reliability of Scripture? List any doubts or questions you may want to investigate.

What do you think of the statement "Fulfilled prophecy is a fact we can analyze and verify. Either it has occurred or it has not"?

In what ways does fulfilled prophecy give you greater confidence in God and the Bible?

Notice that God attaches his character to the accuracy of Bible prophecy. Why is this significant?

Does fulfilled prophecy give you confidence in the other claims in the Bible?

APPLICATION / FURTHER STUDY

What will you take away from today's study? How will it influence you, practically speaking?

What is one prophecy or prophetic category that you would like to investigate further?

PRAYER

LORD, I know your Word says it is impossible to please you without faith (Hebrews 11:6), but it is faith based on facts and supported by evidence. Fulfilled prophecy verifies Scripture and gives me confidence that your Word can be trusted. Help me to embrace this truth as I place my faith in your promises. In Jesus's name, amen.

LESSON 3

Interpretation Methods

(The Non-Prophet's Guide™ to the End Times, Chapter 5)

When I was a new believer, while listening to the radio one day, I stumbled across a preacher who was very confident in what he taught about the end times. He seemed knowledgeable about the Bible and came across as so authoritative that it was easy to adopt his convictions even though I questioned the logic of some of his conclusions. Years later I realized that he was mixing interpretation methods. Sometimes he would use a literal interpretation method, while other times he would allegorize passages and force-fit his preferred meanings into his conclusions.

There are many important things to understand when studying prophecy, and using the correct interpretation method is of prime importance. It is easy to misinterpret Scripture if we allegorize or spiritualize the text. As stated in my book, the literal or futurist interpretation method is the only means by which we can interpret the Bible consistently from cover to cover. I believe this is the most important factor in rightly unlocking scriptural truth—particularly as it relates to our future with Jesus. He is a big God. He knows how to communicate clearly. God says what he means and means what he says.

Although passages of Scripture can have levels of meaning and application, the primary understanding of the text should come through a literal interpretation. If the plain sense of the text is clear, it should be taken at face value. If figures of speech are used, their plain meaning should be fairly obvious—especially when read in their biblical context and when compared with other uses of the words or phrases in Scripture. But in Revelation 20, where we read six times that we will reign with Jesus for 1,000 years in a future earthly kingdom, there is no reason to interpret this as symbolism or allegory. We should interpret this passage literally. To be sure, the Bible makes use of many symbols. Yet these symbols are to be understood by their immediate or broader context—not by our own ideas (2 Peter 1:20).

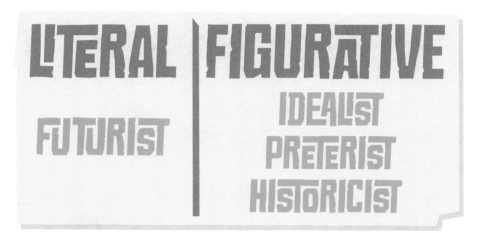

VERSES TO CONSIDER

He gives wisdom to the wise and knowledge to the discerning.
He reveals deep and hidden things; he knows what lies in darkness,
and light dwells with him.

—DANIEL 2:21-22

There is a God in heaven who reveals mysteries.

—DANIEL 2:28

God is not the author of confusion.

—1 CORINTHIANS 14:33 [NKJV]

He will cover you with his feathers, and under his wings you will find
refuge; his faithfulness will be your shield and rampart.

—PSALM 91:4

How does an understanding of interpretation methods help give you confidence when you study God's Word?

Does the literal interpretation method seem most biblical to you? Why or why not?

What do you think the Holy Spirit's role is when we study Scripture?

Do you believe God intends to communicate clearly with us?

Why do you think some Scripture passages require careful study in order for us to understand them?

A paraphrase of the golden rule of interpretation states, "When the plain sense of Scripture makes common sense, seek no other sense, lest it result in nonsense." How is this related to a literal interpretation of Scripture?

How can a spiritualized or allegorized interpretation of Scripture lead to nonsense?

What is one end-time detail or passage that you struggle to believe literally? Or, what is one symbol or statement about prophecy or the last days that confuses you?

Use a concordance or an online Bible tool to see where else in Scripture that symbol or phrase is mentioned and note the surrounding context. Write your observations below.

PRAYER

LORD, as I move further into this study, please help me to discern the best way to approach your Word so that I can properly understand it. Please give me eyes to see and ears to hear as I attempt to properly interpret the clear and intended meaning of Scripture. In Jesus's name, amen.

LESSON 4

Views of the Rapture

(The Non-Prophet's Guide™ to the End Times, Chapter 6)

A recent teaching has crept onto the eschatological scene that says there is, in fact, no rapture. Just today, while doing some research, I bumped into yet another teacher with a lot of letters after his name who claims the doctrine of the rapture was created out of thin air in the 1800s. Nothing could be further from the truth. There are many early church examples of the rapture being taught—not to mention the fact that Paul himself clearly taught about the rapture (see verses below)! Paul

THE RAPTURE ACCORDING TO PAUL & JESUS

1 THESSALONIANS 4:16-17	JOHN 14:3
For the Lord himself will come down from heaven,	And if I go and prepare a place for you,
...the dead in Christ will rise first. After that, we who are still alive and are left will be caught up together with them in the clouds to meet the Lord in the air.	I will come back and take you to be with me
And so we will be with the Lord forever.	that you also may be where I am.

learned the details of the rapture when he was himself "caught up" to heaven to learn the mysteries that God wanted to more fully reveal during the church age (1 Corinthians 15:8; 2 Corinthians 12:2). Some Bible scholars believe this most likely occurred when Paul was stoned and left for dead (Acts 14:19).

With the mystery of the rapture revealed in the New Testament letters, we can also look back and see how the concept was hidden in plain sight once the full revelation of the doctrine was explained (see Psalms 27:5; 57:1; Song of Solomon 2:10-13; Isaiah 26:19-21; and Zephaniah 2:3, for example). The rapture was in the Old Testament concealed and in the New Testament revealed.

For teachers to claim that there is no rapture is a great error at best and outright heretical deception at worst.

HARPAZO IN GREEK

RAPTURO IN LATIN

RAPTURE

HARPAZO = "CAUGHT UP"

VERSES TO CONSIDER

Listen, I tell you a mystery: We will not all sleep, but we will all be changed—in a flash, in the twinkling of an eye, at the last trumpet. For the trumpet will sound, the dead will be raised imperishable, and we will be changed. For the perishable must clothe itself with the imperishable, and the mortal with immortality.

—1 CORINTHIANS 15:51-53

The Lord himself will come down from heaven, with a loud command, with the voice of the archangel and with the trumpet call of God, and the dead in Christ will rise first. After that, we who are still alive and are left will be caught up together with them in the clouds to meet the Lord in the air. And so we will be with the Lord forever.

—1 THESSALONIANS 4:16-17

The grace of God that brings salvation has appeared to all men, teaching us that, denying ungodliness and worldly lusts, we should live soberly, righteously, and godly in the present age, looking for the blessed hope and glorious appearing of our great God and Savior Jesus Christ.

—TITUS 2:11-13 [NKJV]

STUDY QUESTIONS

Does the Lord's future return seem distant or irrelevant? Why or why not?

Why do you think the Lord may have kept the details of the rapture a mystery until after the cross?

After studying the three main views of the rapture, which one seems to fit Scripture the best? Why?

Is the rapture on your mind daily? Why or why not?

Why do you think the doctrine of the rapture is under attack in our day?

APPLICATION / FURTHER STUDY

Think about the details of the rapture and remember that every detail is important. What detail or details are you curious about? How can you investigate them further?

Look up 1 Thessalonians 4:16-17 in an online Greek lexicon and study the meaning behind some of the words—particularly the Greek word translated "caught up." Read the various nuances of the meaning. How does this shed light on the rapture?

LORD, as I study the doctrine of the rapture, help me to better understand its details, timing, purpose, and result. Help me to live as if you were to come today. Help me to live with a sense of excitement and expectation as I work hard and occupy until you come. In Jesus's name, amen.

LESSON 5

Strength of the Pre-Trib Position

(The Non-Prophet's Guide™ to the End Times, Chapter 7)

In chapter 7 you'll find five gigantic pillars that support the pre-trib position.

- We are not appointed to wrath
- Patterns and types
- The Jewish wedding traditions
- Focus on Israel
- 2 Thessalonians 2

I highly recommend you take the time to carefully study each of those reasons as you consider the pre-trib position. In 1 Corinthians 13:12, Paul tells us that we currently see through a glass darkly or see in a dim mirror. Even with all of the prophecies and the 66 books of the Bible, we still see only the highlights. We see only part of the picture. The word "dimly" in this verse literally means "a riddle." It's the Greek word *ainigmati*, which means "to speak in riddles." It comes from the root word *ainigma*, which means "a riddle." This word has made its way into the English language. When something is mysterious or puzzling, we might say it is an enigma.

The reason I bring this up here is because, although I am firmly in the pre-trib camp, there are some very smart people who hold other views. In the book I share five key reasons I believe the pre-trib view is correct, but I want to say that we should be respectful of other views, unite around the fundamentals of the faith, and be careful not to divide over secondary issues. Secondary does not mean unimportant, but my point is that our view of the timing of the rapture is not a salvation issue. It is not an issue we should separate fellowship over.

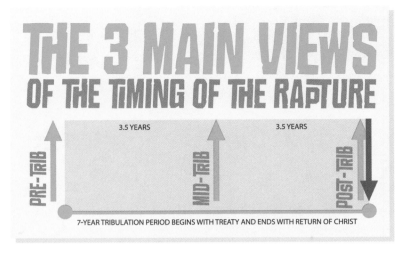

THE 3 MAIN VIEWS OF THE TIMING OF THE RAPTURE

PRE-TRIB | 3.5 YEARS | MID-TRIB | 3.5 YEARS | POST-TRIB

7-YEAR TRIBULATION PERIOD BEGINS WITH TREATY AND ENDS WITH RETURN OF CHRIST

With that said, I'd like to share two other reasons I hold to the pre-trib view that I didn't have room for in the book. First is the doctrine of imminence. In several passages where the Lord's return is mentioned, we find the idea that it could happen at any moment with no preconditions. God knows the exact moment of this glorious future event, and we are told to watch and be ready for it. *Imminent* sounds a lot like "any minute," and though it is not a direct translation, it helps us remember what the word means. From our current perspective, the rapture could literally happen at any minute! This exciting news leads us to the second bonus reason that shows the strength of the pre-trib position.

Titus 2:13 says, "We wait for the blessed hope—the appearing of the glory of our great God and Savior, Jesus Christ." The rapture is known as our "blessed hope"! The prospect of the rapture should give us daily encouragement as we look forward to the moment when we will be changed into our glorified physical state and snatched up to be with Christ—never to be apart from him again! Logically, this can only be true of the pre-trib position. Jesus's appearing is our blessed hope because he is coming to rescue his bride before God's judgment falls on earth. The tribulation period—both halves of it—will be hell on earth. Our blessed hope rescues us from that!

THE BLESSED HOPE!

VERSES TO CONSIDER

God did not appoint us to suffer wrath but to receive salvation through our Lord Jesus Christ.

—1 THESSALONIANS 5:9

Since we have now been justified by his blood, how much more shall we be saved from God's wrath through him!

—ROMANS 5:9

Jesus...rescues us from the coming wrath.

—1 THESSALONIANS 1:10

Because you have kept My command to persevere, I also will keep you from the hour of trial which shall come upon the whole world, to test those who dwell on the earth.

—REVELATION 3:10 (NKJV)

STUDY QUESTIONS

How does it make you feel to know that believers are not appointed to wrath? Do you think that only applies to the afterlife, or to the future end-time judgment as well?

How is it that God is a God of grace but also a God of wrath? Would God truly be a God of love if he let evil go unpunished? Why or why not?

What parallels between Jewish wedding traditions and the rapture stood out to you?

What is the significance of the absence of the word *church* after Revelation chapter 3?

How does the seventieth week in Daniel 9 let us know the focus of the tribulation period is Israel, not the church?

Why is it so important that God keeps his covenant promises to Israel and the Jewish people?

How is that directly related to the promises God has made to those of us who are Gentile believers?

Titus 2:13 calls the rapture our "blessed hope." If the pre-tribulation view is not correct, would it be possible for us to call the rapture our blessed hope? Why or why not?

Do you think the departure spoken of in 2 Thessalonians 2 is a spiritual departure or a physical one? Why?

Do you think 2 Thessalonians 2 could be a double prophecy (referring to the rapture and a great falling away)?

How is this a strong support for the pre-tribulation position if it is talking about a literal, physical departure?

Was it surprising to discover the parallels between end-time events and patterns and types in other accounts of God's judgment (Genesis 6 with Noah, and Genesis 19:12-13 with Lot)? If you have time, read these accounts. Which one stood out to you the most, and why?

Look up these verses in the Old Testament in light of what you know about the rapture. Do you think these are describing the rapture? Record your impressions next to each passage.

Psalm 27:5:

Psalm 57:1:

Isaiah 26:20-21:

Zephaniah 2:3:

PRAYER

LORD, above all else, I want to honor you and I want to know truth. Help me to follow truth wherever it may lead. In view of the trying times in which we live, help me to rejoice in our blessed hope. I long for your return, Lord. Please come soon, and please help me to be full of joy as I wait. In the meantime, as imperfect as I am, help me to work hard to share the good news of salvation and to live a victorious Christian life. In Jesus's name, amen.

LESSON 6

Views of the Millennium

(The Non-Prophet's Guide™ to the End Times, Chapter 8)

As we've seen, a literal approach to the interpretation of Scripture is the only way to interpret all of Scripture in a consistent manner. This approach (with exceptions made for figures of speech and clear symbolism) helps us understand that God's future millennial kingdom is a literal kingdom. After 7 years of hell on earth, there will come 1,000 years of heaven on earth. This 1,000 is not merely a symbolic or unspecified time period. It has theological underpinnings. For reasons hinted at in Scripture but only fully known to God, Satan must be bound for 1,000 years before he is cast into the Lake of Fire forever. Satan has to serve time as a criminal—much like the rebellious angels of Genesis 6 (see also 2 Peter 2:4 and Jude 6)—before receiving his spiritual death penalty. I don't pretend to understand all of the reasons for this 1,000-year binding of Satan while we rule and reign with Christ, but one day, that information will be crystal clear to everyone.

Aside from understanding God's purposes for establishing this time period, there is one major reason it must occur: because God promised it. He promised specific details of a future earthly reign to the Jewish believers in the Old Testament, and he promised it (in various details) to church-age believers (that's us) in the New Testament. He proclaimed this scriptural promise statement with six giant exclamation points. In Revelation chapter 20, the specific time period of 1,000 years is mentioned six times in the first seven verses. There is no hint that this is symbolism or hyperbole.

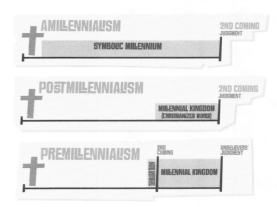

I am reminded of when Jesus asked Peter three times if he loved him. He was driving a point home. When God mentions something more than once, he's trying to get our attention. If he mentions it six times in a short passage, he is really trying to get our attention. It's as if he was saying to us, "Hey, just so we're clear on this—you guys are going to reign with me for one thousand years on earth. Did I mention that? One thousand years, okay? Any questions?" Human ideas often mess up God's clear teaching. He knows our propensity for this. He wanted this point to be abundantly clear. I think he did a great job of doing so.

VERSES TO CONSIDER

He seized the dragon, that ancient serpent, who is the devil, or Satan, and bound him for a thousand years. He threw him into the Abyss, and locked and sealed it over him, to keep him from deceiving the nations anymore until the thousand years were ended. After that, he must be set free for a short time.

—REVELATION 20:2-3

They gathered around him and asked him, "Lord, are you at this time going to restore the kingdom to Israel?"

—ACTS 1:6

STUDY QUESTIONS

Which of the three views makes the most sense to you when reading the Scripture text?

Do you agree that Revelation 20:1-6 supports the fact of Christ's literal 1,000-year reign on earth? Why or why not?

Based on this passage, is it safe to say that the disciples were expecting a literal and physical earthly kingdom?

Jesus also said the kingdom is within us. What do you think he meant by that?

In what way is Satan currently and clearly not bound?

How do you think your current obedience, life experience, trials, victories, talents, and spiritual gifts will play into your role of service in the millennial kingdom?

What can we do now to prepare for the moment we stand before the Lord (believer's judgment/bema seat) to receive our rewards? How might these rewards equip us for service in the kingdom and beyond?

How does that understanding help us serve God better today?

APPLICATION / FURTHER STUDY

Look up these Old Testament verses about the millennial kingdom and think through how they can only be fulfilled in a literal kingdom. Make notes about your observations.

Isaiah 2:1-4:

Jeremiah 23:5-6:

Amos 9:11-12:

Micah 5:2-5:

Zephaniah 3:14-20:

If you would like to dig deeper into this topic, identify a specific area or question to study. Do your own research using online commentaries, lexicons/word studies, and inductive studies to learn more.

LORD, *I don't understand all the details, but I can't wait to rule and reign with you! I want nothing more than to serve you with the gifts, talents, life experience, and passions that you have given me. In the meantime, help me to serve you now. Give me boldness and passion. Help my heart beat for the things that please you, Lord. In Jesus's name, amen.*

LESSON 7

THE BOOK OF DANIEL

LESSON 7

The Book of Daniel

(The Non-Prophet's Guide™ to the End Times, Chapter 10)

For us to understand the book of Revelation, we must also pay attention to the book of Daniel. If you were to take a course on Revelation or eschatology, the book of Daniel would be required reading. As I point out in my book, Daniel is the Revelation of the Old Testament. Every student of eschatology should have a working knowledge of Daniel.

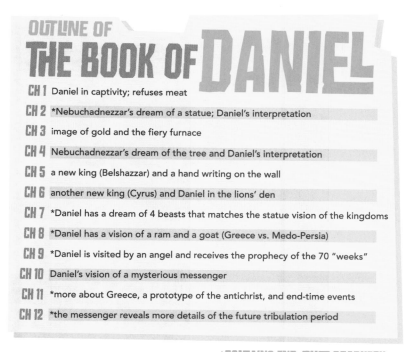

OUTLINE OF THE BOOK OF DANIEL

CH 1 Daniel in captivity; refuses meat

CH 2 *Nebuchadnezzar's dream of a statue; Daniel's interpretation

CH 3 image of gold and the fiery furnace

CH 4 Nebuchadnezzar's dream of the tree and Daniel's interpretation

CH 5 a new king (Belshazzar) and a hand writing on the wall

CH 6 another new king (Cyrus) and Daniel in the lions' den

CH 7 *Daniel has a dream of 4 beasts that matches the statue vision of the kingdoms

CH 8 *Daniel has a vision of a ram and a goat (Greece vs. Medo-Persia)

CH 9 *Daniel is visited by an angel and receives the prophecy of the 70 "weeks"

CH 10 Daniel's vision of a mysterious messenger

CH 11 *more about Greece, a prototype of the antichrist, and end-time events

CH 12 *the messenger reveals more details of the future tribulation period

*CONTAINS END-TIMES PROPHECY

What would you think if I told you that Daniel is more relevant now than when it was written? Daniel 12:4 and 9 confirm that the prophecies given to Daniel would not be understood (unsealed) until the time of the end. A careful study of church history shows that in the 1600s (after the Reformation and specifically with the Puritans and other believers of that era), a renewed interest in the book of Daniel slowly emerged. People started teaching that Israel would become a nation again and it happened—during the same period when knowledge and travel exploded (Daniel 12:4). Now, in our day, we see all the conditions Daniel (and John) predicted taking shape. The book of Daniel is unsealed.

Consider this: The closer you get to the impact site of an airplane crash, the more debris you will find. The closer you get to a destination you've read about, the more you will understand its layout as you see the terrain and take in all the sights and sounds. I believe the closer we get to the rapture and all that follows, the better we will understand the book of Daniel and other eschatological passages of Scripture.

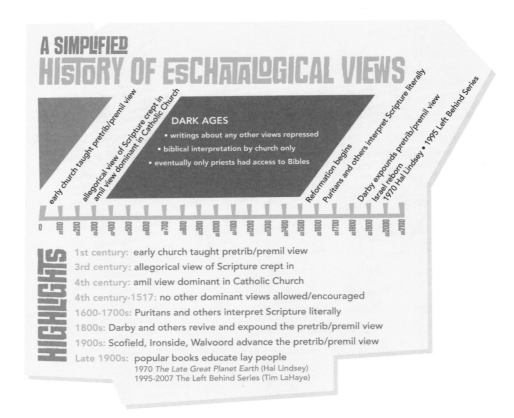

A SIMPLIFIED
HISTORY OF ESCHATALOGICAL VIEWS

early church taught pretrib/premil view
allegorical view of Scripture crept in
amil view dominant in Catholic Church

DARK AGES
• writings about any other views repressed
• biblical interpretation by church only
• eventually only priests had access to Bibles

Reformation begins
Puritans and others interpret Scripture literally
Darby expounds pretrib/premil view
Israel reborn
1970 Hal Lindsey • 1995 Left Behind Series

0 AD100 AD200 AD300 AD400 AD500 AD600 AD700 AD800 AD900 AD1000 AD1100 AD1200 AD1300 AD1400 AD1500 AD1600 AD1700 AD1800 AD1900 AD2000 AD2100

HIGHLIGHTS

1st century: early church taught pretrib/premil view
3rd century: allegorical view of Scripture crept in
4th century: amil view dominant in Catholic Church
4th century-1517: no other dominant views allowed/encouraged
1600-1700s: Puritans and others interpret Scripture literally
1800s: Darby and others revive and expound the pretrib/premil view
1900s: Scofield, Ironside, Walvoord advance the pretrib/premil view
Late 1900s: popular books educate lay people
1970 *The Late Great Planet Earth* (Hal Lindsey)
1995-2007 The Left Behind Series (Tim LaHaye)

VERSES TO CONSIDER

He gave me this explanation: "The fourth beast is a fourth kingdom that will appear on earth. It will be different from all the other kingdoms and will devour the whole earth, trampling it down and crushing it."

—DANIEL 7:23

Seventy "sevens" are decreed for your people and your holy city to finish transgression, to put an end to sin, to atone for wickedness, to bring in everlasting righteousness, to seal up vision and prophecy and to anoint the Most Holy Place.

—DANIEL 9:24

You, Daniel, roll up and seal the words of the scroll until the time of the end. Many will go here and there to increase knowledge.

—DANIEL 12:4

Go your way, Daniel, because the words are rolled up and sealed until the time of the end.

—DANIEL 12:9

STUDY QUESTIONS

Read Daniel 7, and note the similarities and differences with Daniel 2.

What did you learn about the antichrist from the book of Daniel?

What symbolism did you see in the book of Daniel that connects to Revelation and other end-time passages? (Example: horns representing power, etc.)

What two entities does the prophecy in Daniel 9:24 focus on?

What does this say about God's view of the Jewish people and the city of Jerusalem?

How do God's unconditional promises to Abraham—the father of the Jewish race—relate to Daniel 9:24?

Do you see the gap in Daniel's vision (which we now know is the church age) between the destruction of one temple (verse 26) and the existence of a new one (verse 27)?

Why do you think God kept the church age concealed in the Old Testament?

APPLICATION / FURTHER STUDY

Review the five things we learn from the seventy-weeks prophecy as stated on pages 110-111 of *The Non-Prophet's Guide™ to the End Times*. Note anything that stands out that you may want to study in greater depth, and record your notes below.

LORD, in the spirit of Daniel I come to you in humility and repentance. I confess my sins and the sins of your people. As believers we often fall short and get sidetracked by worldly things. Forgive us, Lord, and help us to submit to you at this critical time in history.

Like Daniel, I want to seek your will, your Word, and your ways. Unseal this amazing book to me, Lord, and help me to understand our times. Use me like you used Daniel, who lived in the midst of a pagan culture far away from his home. I too feel stuck in a pagan world system away from my true home. Help me to be in the world but not of the world. Help me to avoid the traps laid by the enemy so I can be used mightily by you. Guide my steps and use me as you see fit. I pray all of this in the name of Jesus, my Lord and Savior. Amen.

LESSON 8

THE OLIVET DISCOURSE

LESSON 8

The Olivet Discourse

(The Non-Prophet's Guide™ to the End Times, Chapter 11)

One matter I didn't have space to discuss very much in *The Non-Prophet's Guide™ to the End Times* is the fact that there are a few issues that prophecy experts disagree on with regard to our understanding of the Olivet Discourse. For example, there is much discussion about the meaning of what Jesus said in the parable of the fig tree. The big question here is this:

Does the fig tree in Matthew 24:32-35 represent Israel?

Take a few minutes to read Matthew 24:32-35, Mark 13:28-31, and Luke 21:29-32. These three passages record Jesus's teaching about the fig tree. The passage in Matthew is viewed as the primary text when it comes to discussing the topic.

In Jeremiah 24, we clearly see Israel described, in parable form, as a basket of good and bad figs (see also 1 Kings 4:25 and Zechariah 3:10). As we adhere to the principle of letting Scripture interpret Scripture, these Old Testament precedents shed light on what the fig tree represents in the Matthew account.

In Matthew 21, as Jesus was headed into Jerusalem, he came across a fig tree. This incident took place after several key events during the passion week, including the triumphal entry, the clearing of the temple courts, and Jesus being rejected by the religious leaders. Immediately after this last incident, we read the following in Matthew 21:18-19: "Early in the morning, as Jesus was on his way back to the city, he was hungry. Seeing a fig tree by the road, he

went up to it but found nothing on it except leaves. Then he said to it, 'May you never bear fruit again!' Immediately the tree withered."

Here, Jesus used parables in his interaction with the religious leaders to condemn them. After entering the city on a donkey and being rejected by the religious leaders, he cursed the fig tree for being barren. The next time we see the religious leaders in the narrative, they are plotting Jesus's arrest and death. Note also what Jesus told them in Matthew 21:43, when he said, "I tell you that the kingdom of God will be taken away from you and given to a people who will produce its fruit."

After this and several other condemning parables and a direct indictment against the leaders in chapter 23, Jesus ended with this heartbreaking proclamation in Matthew 23:37-39: "Jerusalem, Jerusalem, you who kill the prophets and stone those sent to you, how often I have longed to gather your children together, as a hen gathers her chicks under her wings, and you were not willing. Look, your house is left to you desolate. For I tell you, you will not see me again until you say, 'Blessed is he who comes in the name of the Lord.'"

This sequence of events, demonstrating how Israel's rejection of the Messiah led to their house being left desolate, syncs with the symbolism of a cursed and withered fig tree, as well as to the next reference to a fig tree blooming—yet without fruit—as the world approaches the last days. That is, the context and chronological flow of Matthew 21–24 supports the idea of the fig tree in Matthew 24 being representative of Israel.

This notion is further supported by key passages about Israel's rebirth. For example, in Ezekiel 37, in the prophet's vision of the valley of dry bones, Israel is seen as coming back to life in two phases—first alive but without God's Spirit, then finally with God's Spirit and knowing that it was the Lord's doing (Ezekiel 37:1-14). This mirrors the Matthew 24 account, in which we see the fig tree coming to life but without fruit. First comes the revived national state, then later—at the end of the tribulation—all Israel will accept Christ (Romans 11:26) when the people say, "Blessed is he who comes in the name of the Lord" (Matthew 23:39).

EZEKIEL 37

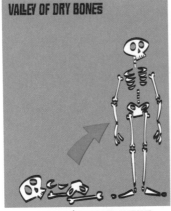

VALLEY OF DRY BONES

ISRAEL SCATTERED | HOMELAND DESOLATE

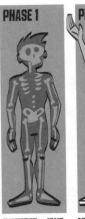

PHASE 1

GATHERED TO LAND IN UNBELIEF

PHASE 2

ALL ISRAEL SAVED
EZEKIEL 37:14; MATTHEW 23:39; ROMANS 11:26

Do you think it's natural for people to want to know when the end will come?

If you were to have a private meeting with Jesus about the end times, what three questions would you ask him?

Why is it significant that Jesus didn't rebuke his disciples for asking about the time of his return?

In the Olivet Discourse, note that the first end-time sign Jesus mentioned was deception (Matthew 24:4). How important is it that we guard the truth?

As you read through Matthew 24, what signs stood out to you the most, and why?

Do you agree that the fig tree blossoming represents Israel becoming a nation again? Why or why not?

What time period do you believe Matthew 24:36-41 is describing—prior to the rapture, or immediately before the second coming of Christ to destroy his enemies at the end of the tribulation period?

LORD, thank you for providing so many details about what the end times will look like. Open my spiritual eyes and ears as I study the details of your teaching as given to the disciples. You masterfully answered their questions in a way that was immediately relevant to them and prophetically relevant to us almost 2,000 years later. Help me to understand the relevance of the Olivet discourse for today and to understand the signs preceding your return. Equip me to endure these challenging times with an eye toward the sky. In Jesus's name I pray. Amen.

LESSON 9

The Book of Revelation

(The Non-Prophet's Guide™ to the End Times, Chapter 12)

The more we are familiar with the framework of Daniel and the incredible details shared by Jesus in the Olivet Discourse, the more the book of Revelation makes sense. Without the help of these prophetic portions of Scripture, Revelation would be more difficult to understand, and some readers would probably even conclude that it's just a confusing apocalyptic work by a crazy old man who had too much time on his hands. But because Revelation is part of the Holy Spirit-inspired canon, we know it was given by God to provide for us a more complete picture of what he wants us to know about the future.

It's sad that there are a few popular movements within evangelical Christianity that minimize the importance and application of the Old Testament. Put bluntly, this is dangerous ground. It is error at best; it is "doctrines of demons" (1 Timothy 4:1) at worst. Revelation—the capstone of Scripture and crescendo of history—can't be understood without a working knowledge of and respect for the Old Testament.

Revelation contains 404 verses with more than 800 allusions to the Old Testament. It assumes a working knowledge of the history, prophecy, and application of the Old Testament. When Paul wrote that "all Scripture is God-breathed and is useful for teaching, rebuking, correcting and training in righteousness" (2 Timothy 3:16), the only Scripture available at the time *was* the Old Testament.

What's more, there is a continuous link between Genesis, where key Bible themes are introduced, and Revelation, where we learn about the future fulfillment of all things prophetic.

VERSES TO CONSIDER

Write, therefore, what you have seen, what is now and what will take place later.

—REVELATION 1:19

Blessed is the one who reads aloud the words of this prophecy, and blessed are those who hear it and take to heart what is written in it, because the time is near.

—REVELATION 1:3

The Spirit clearly says that in later times some will abandon the faith and follow deceiving spirits and things taught by demons.

—1 TIMOTHY 4:1

STUDY QUESTIONS

How does Revelation 1:19 help lay out the book chronologically? Does this verse take some of the mystery and confusion away and give you a sense for how the book plays out?

Study the basic outline chart on page 126 of *The Non-Prophet's Guide™ to the End Times*. Do the chapter descriptions help provide further chronological details about the book?

What new things have you learned about the chronology of the book of Revelation?

Do you think the symbolism in Revelation can be understood? Why or why not?

How important do you think it is to understand and apply the life lessons provided in the Old Testament?

With regard to the movements in our day to discredit the Old Testament—how does this cause confusion among Christians about the relevance of the Bible's final book?

APPLICATION / FURTHER STUDY

As an exercise, pick one symbol that seems confusing or unclear to you. Using a concordance, look up other usages of that symbol (or word) in Scripture. Each time you look up that symbol or word, what is the context? What is the symbol or word related to? In what ways do the other passages help shine more light on the one that seems confusing?

PRAYER

LORD, as I study Bible prophecy, help me to gain a broad understanding of its key themes as they are progressively revealed in the Old and New Testaments. Give me an ever-deepening confidence in every nuance of the Scriptures as I keep in mind the fact that you sovereignly ordained its writing, assembly, and transmission to us. Give me a desire to learn more about John's Revelation, about the church age, and the end times. Use your Word to ignite a fire in me to share my faith as we draw closer to your Son's return. In Jesus's name, amen.

LESSON 10

SIGNS OF THE END TIMES

LESSON 10

Signs of the End Times

(*The Non-Prophet's Guide™ to the End Times,* Chapter 13)

When Jesus's disciples asked him what signs to look for so they would know when the end of the church age was approaching, rather than rebuke them, Jesus gave a full chapter's worth of signs followed by another full chapter of related parables. This central teaching by Jesus regarding the end-time signs, known as the Olivet Discourse, is recorded in three of the four Gospels—in Matthew 24, Mark 13, and Luke 21. It is the second-longest recorded teaching by Jesus.

Hebrews 10:25 exhorts us to not give up "meeting together, as some are in the habit of doing, but [to encourage] one another—and all the more as you see the Day approaching." That "Day" is "the day of the Lord," or what is also known as the tribulation period and arrival of God's kingdom. This verse plainly tells us that those who are taking notice will be able to see this time period drawing close.

Some Christians have reservations about the idea we might be able to tell when Christ's return is near because of the admonition in 1 Thessalonians 5:2 that tells us "the day of the Lord will come like a thief in the night." But the mistake they make is to stop right there. Just two verses later, we read a crystal-clear proclamation that believers *will not be* caught by surprise. In verses 4-6, we read, "You, brothers and sisters, are not in darkness so that this day should surprise you like a thief. You are all children of the light and children of the day. We do not belong to the night or to the darkness. So then, let us not be like others, who are asleep, but let us be awake and sober."

Friend, that is as clear as Scripture gets. We are admonished to not sleep but to remain awake and to keep watching! Please don't overlook the importance of these verses. We have clear marching orders to stay awake. The implication is that many will be asleep—it will be tempting to do this, perhaps even understandable (from a human perspective). But we must stay awake, pay attention, and watch for the specific signs Jesus mentioned.

Jesus openly and boldly criticized the religious leaders (the Pharisees and Sadducees) and the crowds for not understanding the prophetic nature of their times. His first coming had been clearly prophesied in the Old Testament books, yet upon his arrival, many did not recognize who he was. Some individuals, however, had been alert to the signs and realized that he was the Messiah—including the wise men, Simeon, Anna, and John the Baptist.

VERSES TO CONSIDER

To the religious leaders Jesus said, "You know how to interpret the weather signs in the sky, but you don't know how to interpret the signs of the times!"

—MATTHEW 16:3 (NLT)

To the crowds he said, "You fools! You know how to interpret the weather signs of the earth and sky, but you don't know how to interpret the present times."

—LUKE 12:56 (NLT)

...not giving up meeting together, as some are in the habit of doing, but encouraging one another—and all the more as you see the Day approaching.

—HEBREWS 10:25

STUDY QUESTIONS

In what ways have you seen the concept of end-time signs abused or sensationalized?

In what ways have you seen the concept of end-time signs neglected or mocked?

What are your thoughts about the truth in 1 Thessalonians 5:1-11 that some will be caught off guard by the rapture and others will not?

What do you think are the main reasons people didn't recognize who Jesus was at his first coming?

What do you think are the main reasons people don't recognize the signs in our day?

What can we learn from those who were watching when Jesus came the first time?

APPLICATION / FURTHER STUDY

In one or two sittings, read 1 and 2 Thessalonians and notice how thoroughly the concept of the Lord's return was interwoven with Paul's instructions to this group of recent converts.

PRAYER

LORD, help me to live every day with a sense of anticipation and watch-fulness. Though we don't know the day or hour of your return, and though we're not guaranteed you will come in our lifetime, we know that the rapture is nearer now than it has ever been. Help me to live with this awareness daily as I watch and wait. Also, help me to work hard and occupy until you come — with the attitude of an ambassador who is living away from my true home. In Jesus's name, amen.

LESSON 11

THE SUPER SIGN

LESSON 11

The Super Sign

(*The Non-Prophet's Guide™ to the End Times*, Chapter 13)

In chapter 10 of *The Non-Prophet's Guide™ to the End Times*, we looked at the prophecies in the book of Daniel and noted that in the 70-weeks prophecy, God's plan for the Jewish people was to occur over the first 69 sets of 7 years. With the birth of the church in Acts 2, the Jewish prophetic clock paused for the church age. At some future point in time, the church will be taken out of the picture via the rapture. Soon after, the tribulation period will begin when the antichrist signs or enforces a treaty with Israel. This event will cause the Jewish prophetic clock to start again in order to complete the last set of 7 years—which also happens to be the duration of the tribulation period. During this time, God's attention will turn back to the Jews and Israel. He will carry out his work through 2 Jewish witnesses and 144,000 Jewish evangelists, and the entire world will become hyper-focused on Jerusalem and persecuting the Jewish people.

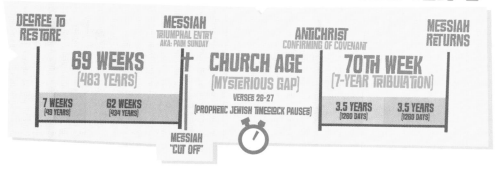

A study of various key prophetic passages (especially Ezekiel 37–40) demonstrates that although the Jews are God's chosen people, most of them won't accept Christ until the end of the tribulation (Matthew 23:39; Romans 9:27-29). Some passages also indicate that a small remnant will turn to Christ before the tribulation when they are back in their

homeland. That's exactly what we've seen happening today. If you keep this in mind as you study Bible prophecy, the puzzle pieces will continue to fall in place and you'll have a clearer understanding of God's plans for the future.

After Jerusalem was destroyed in AD 70 by Rome and the Jewish people were dispersed to the surrounding lands, some 1,800 years went by with only a small Jewish remnant living in Israel. During that entire period there was an extended drought—Israel became a vast wasteland. By the twentieth century, there were far fewer trees left in the region, and there were no trees south of the Sea of Galilee. To make matters worse, the Ottoman Turks taxed trees, so the inhabitants in the land cut them down to avoid paying taxes. Erosion and stagnant water led to the formation of swamps, which, in turn, produced widespread malaria. Because of these conditions, nobody wanted this land.

> Deuteronomy 28:23-24—The sky over your head will be bronze, the ground beneath you iron. The Lord will turn the rain of your country into dust and powder; it will come down from the skies until you are destroyed.

The American author Mark Twain, who was a world traveler, visited Israel in 1866. He stated in his journal that while riding on horseback through the Jezreel Valley, he and his travel group saw "not a solitary village throughout its whole extent—not for 30 miles in either direction. There are two or three small clusters of Bedouin tents, but not a single permanent habitation. One may ride 10 miles, hereabouts, and not see 10 human beings."[1] Twain described the region as the most desolate wasteland imaginable.

But soon after Israel's rebirth in 1948, weather patterns shifted, the Jewish residents worked diligently, and today, Israel is a lush and fruitful land that exports crops, cutting-edge technology, and (beginning in 2017) gas and oil. For several decades after Israel's rebirth, only small amounts of gas and oil were found in the small country. Then a few years ago, massive gas and oil reserves were discovered. In my opinion, the timing is not mere coincidence. These finds lay the groundwork for the fulfillment of several end-time prophecies.

MARK TWAIN

Earlier I mentioned that the Puritans of the 1600s, among others, returned to a literal understanding of Bible prophecy. This caused them to believe, preach, and write about Israel's future regathering as predicted in Scripture. For 200 years, most people thought this notion was crazy, but then the first budding of this future fulfillment appeared. The First Zionist congress was held in 1897, the Balfour Declaration was issued in 1917, then in 1947 the United Nations adopted the "Partition of Palestine." This was followed by Israel's rebirth in 1948. All of these key events relate to the budding of the fig tree. Since Israel's rebirth, the rate of prophetic fulfillment has steadily increased with each passing decade—to the point where every key prophetic indicator related to Israel is in active play in our day! Israel is truly the super sign of all end-times Bible prophecy.

VERSES TO CONSIDER

The Lord will scatter you among all nations, from one end of the earth to the other.

—DEUTERONOMY 28:64

In that day the Lord will reach out his hand a second time to reclaim the surviving remnant of his people.

—ISAIAH 11:11

The Lord gave another message to Jeremiah. He said, "Have you noticed what people are saying?—'The Lord chose Judah and Israel and then abandoned them!' They are sneering and saying that Israel is not worthy to be counted as a nation. But this is what the Lord says: I would no more reject my people than I would change my laws that govern night and day, earth and sky."

—JEREMIAH 33:23-25 (NLT)

"The days are coming," declares the Lord, "when it will no longer be said, 'As surely as the Lord lives, who brought the Israelites up out of Egypt,' but it will be said, 'As surely as the Lord lives, who brought the Israelites up out of the land of the north and out of all the countries where he had banished them.' For I will restore them to the land I gave their ancestors."

—JEREMIAH 16:14-15

I will take you out of the nations; I will gather you from all the countries and bring you back into your own land.

—EZEKIEL 36:24

> *The desolate land will be cultivated instead of lying desolate in the sight of all who pass through it. They will say, "This land that was laid waste has become like the garden of Eden; the cities that were lying in ruins, desolate and destroyed, are now fortified and inhabited."*
>
> —EZEKIEL 36:34-35

> *This is what the Sovereign LORD says: I will take the Israelites out of the nations where they have gone. I will gather them from all around and bring them back into their own land. I will make them one nation in the land, on the mountains of Israel.*
>
> —EZEKIEL 37:21-22

STUDY QUESTIONS

Think about the millions of details over the past 2,000 years that have had to be worked out to make the prophecies about Israel and the Jewish people come true. In what ways is all this such a great miracle?

Does it seem providential or coincidental to you that Mark Twain traveled to Israel's homeland and recorded the terrible conditions there just before the prophetic winds of Zionism began to blow? How does this historical record verify and align with end-time Bible prophecies related to the events surrounding Israel's rebirth?

How does the fact that every key prophetic indicator related to Israel is in active play right now affect your thoughts about the closeness of end-time events?

Why do you think we are witnessing such a significant rise in global antisemitism in our day?

Why do you think many (if not most) Christians are not aware of Israel's stature as a super sign of the end times?

APPLICATION / FURTHER STUDY

Read Jeremiah 31:1 and Leviticus 26:42-45 slowly and carefully. How were these very early prophecies about Israel and the Jewish people fulfilled?

PRAYER

LORD, I stand in awe at your foreknowledge of future events. It is amazing to me that you predicted the impossible and the impossible came true. When I consider the miracle of Israel and the fact that you predicted her rebirth in the last days in great detail, I can only conclude that you are sovereignly in control of the large and small details of your decrees. Please help more believers awaken to the fact that Israel's rebirth is a super sign that we are nearing the time of your return to set up your kingdom. Help me personally to not lose sight of this amazing fact. In Jesus's name, amen.

LESSON 12

GEOPOLITICAL SIGNS, PART 1

LESSON 12

Geopolitical Signs, Part 1

(The Non-Prophet's Guide™ to the End Times, Chapter 14)

There is a tremendous amount of geopolitical activity taking place in our day that has prophetic implications. We could talk about this for days, but I've limited this discussion to two lessons for the purposes of this study. I've tried to include some key points that were briefly highlighted in the book but could have been discussed at greater length. In this lesson I want to focus on the Middle East and highlight some details related to the war of Gog and Magog, which is described in Ezekiel 38–39.

EZEKIEL 38 NATIONS
AND THEIR MODERN-DAY EQUIVALENTS

ANCIENT NAME	MODERN NAME
MAGOG	RUSSIA, CENTRAL ASIA
ROSH	RUSSIA
MESHECH	RUSSIA
TUBAL	RUSSIA OR TURKEY
PERSIA	IRAN
CUSH	ETHIOPIA, SUDAN
LUD	LIBYA, ALGERIA
GOMER	TURKEY
TOGARMAH	TURKEY, CENTRAL ASIA

Ezekiel 38 Alignment

When?

Most prophecy experts are not dogmatic about when this war will take place; they simply say it will be near the end of this era. As I study prophecy, I tend to think this war will happen as a Mideast power (and natural resource) grab soon after the rapture, or in the very early stages of the tribulation period (perhaps as part of the second seal judgment—the fiery red horse of war).

What Plunder?

While Israel is a supremely successful agricultural, technological, and business start-up country, it has always relied entirely on imported energy sources. Jewish rabbis have often joked that God blessed them with milk and honey but accidentally gave all the oil to the Arabs.

However, in 2009, a natural gas field large enough to fill 40 percent of Israel's energy needs was discovered. The Tamar field, 15 miles off the coast of Israel, was the first of several such fields Israel would go on to discover in 2012 and 2013. But wait—there's more! In 2015, a massive oil reserve ten times larger than average-sized oil fields in other parts of the world was discovered in the Golan Heights.

What that all means in concrete terms is this: Prior to 2009, Israel had to import energy. But now, she is a major exporter of energy. All of this amidst reports that oil production in the surrounding countries will peak in a few short years, and the fact that Israeli energy exports to Europe will cut directly into Russia's oil sales, which are its main source of national funding.

With that in mind, read this telling verse found in the Ezekiel account: "Sheba and Dedan and the merchants of Tarshish and all her villages will say to you, 'Have you come to plunder?'" (Ezekiel 38:13). Sheba and Dedan are modern-day Saudi Arabia, and many prophecy experts believe Tarshish is modern-day England. If that is the case, "her villages"—other translations render this as coastlands—could be seen as America and other countries originally colonized by England.

In other words, Saudi Arabia, England, and America will question this invasion of Israel, and this verse gives us insight into the fact that Russia will be after something of value. Could it be that Russia will attempt to usurp Israel's oil and gas?

Perhaps this factor—along with the partnerships Russia currently has with Iran, Turkey, and other radical Islamic countries that have a satanic hatred for Israel—is the "hook in the jaw" mentioned in Ezekiel 38:4 that God will use to "turn" him around from his country's affairs and draw this end-time Russian leader into war.

Isaiah 17 Destruction

There is one other important prophecy that I should note here. It's found in Isaiah 17 and concerns the destruction of Damascus, a major city in Syria. We read this in verse 1: "See, Damascus will no longer be a city but will become a heap of ruins." And in verse 14 we read, "At evening time, behold, there is terror! Before morning they are no more. Such will be the portion of those who plunder us and the lot of those who pillage us" (NASB).

Damascus is the longest continually inhabited city in existence. Many prophecy experts believe that the sudden destruction of Damascus will be the catalyst that triggers the Ezekiel 38 war, or that it will occur in conjunction with the Ezekiel 38 war. These 2,600-plus-year-old prophecies have not been fulfilled as of yet. Damascus, though ravaged by the Syrian Civil War, still stands and still has people living there.

Iran is setting up shop in Damascus and its mullahs openly state their religiously driven plans to destroy Israel. Ongoing airstrikes since 2017 by Israel against weapons convoys (gifts from Iran to Hezbollah terrorists and other proxies) and Iranian-built missile factories near Damascus make one wonder how close we are to Isaiah 17 and Ezekiel 38. We're not told who will destroy Damascus or how, but the surrounding verses suggest the devastation will occur during a conflict with Israel. Though we are not told that Isaiah 17 will trigger Ezekiel 38, this is a logical (and currently viable) possibility.

Is it sheer coincidence that the Russia-Iran-Turkey alliance has formed around the same time that Israel is becoming energy-independent and discovering massive amounts of potential plunder? I believe we are seeing the stage for the last-days "Gog and Magog War" being set before our very eyes.

STUDY QUESTIONS

Does the realization that geopolitical events are lining up with Bible prophecy make those events more interesting to watch?

How does Bible prophecy help us better understand the spiritual war going on behind the scenes of geopolitics?

Have you noticed how often geopolitical conflict and intrigue points the world's attention to the Middle East? Why do you think this is?

APPLICATION / FURTHER STUDY

Carefully and prayerfully read Ezekiel 38–39, making note of specific details that jump out at you. Then read recent news articles from established Israeli news sites (look for articles related to Syria, Iran, Russia, Turkey, Sudan, and Libya). What impressions do you get about today's events in light of Bible prophecy?

PRAYER

LORD, as we see the Ezekiel 38 war being set up in our day, remind us that the rapture is (most likely) before that monumental event, during which you will openly and miraculously come to the rescue of Israel. Give us eyes to see and ears to hear as we carefully study the events of our day in light of the prophecies in your Word. In Jesus's name, amen.

LESSON 13

Geopolitical Signs, Part 2

(The Non-Prophet's Guide™ to the End Times, Chapter 14)

In the previous lesson, we focused on the Middle East and took a look at some of the key details related to the Ezekiel 38 war. Today, we'll look at another geopolitical alignment that is in active play in our day—one that is related to Europe.

The Ten Toes

In Daniel 2, we read about King Nebuchadnezzar's dream about a great statue made up of gold, silver, bronze, iron, and clay. The different parts of the statue represented successive major kingdoms, beginning with the head of gold, or the kingdom of Babylon. The last state depicted by the statue is the ten toes made up of a mixture of iron and clay. According to Daniel 2:34-35, these toes will be destroyed by a rock "cut out…not by human hands," and this rock will become "a huge mountain" that fills "the whole earth." This rock represents Jesus, who will judge the final world empire and set up his millennial kingdom in fulfillment of many Old Testament prophecies.

We learn from Scripture cross-references that the ten toes of the statue are elite end-time rulers of ten nations or world regions. Later on, in chapter 7, Daniel records another prophetic vision for us. There we find the same four kingdoms, only this time they are seen as beasts, and instead of ten toes, we find ten horns.

QUICK FACT: DID YOU KNOW...
that in the Bible, horns symbolize power and authority?

The final beast (the antichrist) seems to rise to greater power after the ten toes/ten horns are in place. This evil end-time ruler is seen as overtaking three rulers' positions of authority. We read this in Daniel 7:24: "The ten horns are ten kings who will come from this kingdom. After them another king will arise, different from the earlier ones; he will subdue three kings."

We find similar language in Revelation chapters 13 and 17, where the antichrist is seen as ruling three of the ten nations or world regions. For example, in Revelation 13:1 we read, "I saw a beast coming out of the sea. It had ten horns and seven heads, with ten crowns on its horns, and on each head a blasphemous name."

We know from Daniel's 70-weeks prophecy in Daniel 9 that the antichrist will arise from the area where the Roman Empire's seat of power was established. We read in verse 26 that "the people of the ruler who will come will destroy the city and the sanctuary." The people who destroyed Jerusalem and the second temple were the Romans, and this verse informs us that the antichrist will come from those people. Most prophecy experts believe that to mean he will arise from one of the Western European countries.

Some experts believe the antichrist will be a Muslim arising from the Eastern leg of the Roman Empire, but this view doesn't have much support in Scripture. According to Daniel 11:37, the antichrist "will show no regard for the gods of his ancestors...nor will he regard any god." We are also told he will broker a peace deal with Israel and let the Jewish people rebuild their temple. After that, he will declare himself to be God. None of this squares with the idea of the antichrist being a Muslim. Now, back to our regularly scheduled programming.

Is it mere coincidence that the European Union has arisen in the years following Israel's rebirth? If you think pegging the European Union as the revived Roman Empire seen in Daniel 9 is a stretch, consider the upcoming facts.

The Woman Riding a Beast

In Revelation 17, John refers to a prostitute who is riding the beast, or the antichrist. In verse 5, the woman is called "Babylon the Great. The Mother of Prostitutes and of the Abominations of the Earth." This connects back to the Tower of Babel mentioned in Genesis 11. Most pagan and occult practices, as well as Greek and Roman mythologies, have Babylonian roots and can be traced back to Nimrod and the Tower of Babel.

As we consider the fact that the prophecies in Revelation describe an end-time global religion with roots in ancient Babylon, we can take stock of current trends to see whether this end-time condition is beginning to develop. Many people don't realize that there is a growing push today toward a single, all-inclusive religion. Pope Francis and some influential Protestant leaders have openly, directly, and strongly advocated (by words and action) for an all-inclusive acceptance of all world religions and philosophies, including atheism.

With those thoughts in mind, consider this: The EU parliament building in Strasbourg, France, is intentionally designed to look like the famous 1563 painting by Pieter Bruegel depicting the Tower of Babel. This imagery is also used in the EU parliament's design and marketing materials, including posters, postcards, and other official branding pieces.

BRUEGEL'S PAINTING **EU PARLIAMENT BUILDING**

If you do a little research, you'll also find that EU statues, coins, commemorative stamps, and other branding collateral from the EU nations depict a woman riding a beast. This woman, Europa, comes from Greek mythology, and the bull is the Greek god Zeus. The apostle John identified Zeus with Satan in Revelation 2:12-17, saying that "Satan has his throne" in the temple of Zeus at Pergamum (the continent of Europe is said to be named after Europa).

EUROPA BUILDING STATUE
BRUSSELLS, BELGIUM

EUROPEAN PARLIAMENT STATUE
STRASBURG, FRANCE

So, not only has the EU arisen after the rebirth of Israel, but the two key symbols used by the EU link directly to specific symbols presented in the book of Revelation. For these and other reasons, many prophecy experts believe the EU is the infrastructure on which the end-time revived Roman Empire will be built.

One-World Currency

For a one-world currency to exist, the various economic systems of sovereign countries would somehow have to become integrated into a global order. Countries would have to move away from a focus on national financial stability and security toward an interconnected global economy. With the proliferation of electronic banking resources, one could easily imagine the possibility of a completely cashless form of global banking in the near future. Many globalist institutions in Europe and other places have been working toward creating such a system.

The Great Recession of 2008 has already shown us how economically interconnected the world is today. We are now at the point where an economic event in one place will affect all others around the world—which shows just how fragile the global economy has become. For example, in 2016, when British voters passed a referendum in favor of Brexit—the withdrawal of the United Kingdom from the European Union—this caused financial shock waves that were felt all around the world.

The Philippines, Australia, and India all have major cashless developments emerging, and anticash lobbies exist in most countries. Unified currencies such as the Euro, electronic funds transfer, PayPal, Bitcoin, credit card companies, Facebook's GlobalCoin, and other such cashless systems are all paving the way for a cashless society and a one-world currency.

Just to highlight one of these, in 2009, Bitcoin, a cashless decentralized digital currency, was introduced. It was invented by an unknown programmer (or group of programmers) of unknown location going by the fictitious name of Satoshi Nakamoto. This cashless system was made possible through the use of open-source software and is set up so that individuals can make transactions directly without using a bank of any sort. Accounts are kept on a public ledger called a blockchain. Bitcoin has been used in both legal and black-market economies. In other words, a completely cashless system already exists.

Meanwhile, the United Nations, the European Union, and organizations such as the Bilderberg Group and the G8 continue to push toward a global government and one-world currency. These organizations do everything they can to influence our economics, laws, military, and policies toward this goal.

Which geopolitical sign intrigues you the most, and why?

How can we discern between conspiracy theories and verifiable, fact-based developments that line up with end-time geopolitical signs?

Even a few decades ago, many people had never heard of a cashless system. In what ways have you seen cashless systems of currency come into play during your lifetime? How compelling do you feel it is that Revelation predicted such cashless systems almost 2,000 years ago?

APPLICATION / FURTHER STUDY

Do a quick Internet search about a key nation or leader and see what news articles have shown up this week about that country or person. List the developments below. Do you see anything that seems to indicate our world is generally drawing closer to the end times?

Which world leaders or political figures seem to be having the greatest effect on world events right now (for good or bad)? List them below.

LESSON 14

Signs of Nature

(*The Non-Prophet's Guide™ to the End Times*, Chapter 15)

When Jesus taught about the signs of the end times, he spoke of them as occurring in the same way as birth pains—as time goes on, they will increase in frequency and intensity. Among the signs are those connected with nature in some way, such as earthquakes. Jesus also mentioned pestilence, which can include any wide-scale disaster—particularly if it is related to God's judgment. The Greek word translated "pestilence" in the New Testament is *loimos* (loy'-mos) and it can mean "plague," "famine," or "disease." The Olivet Discourse seems to include all three.

In the book of Exodus, God's judgments on Egypt (which were a clear type or foreshadow of end-time judgments) were called plagues. These included water turning into blood, frogs, lice or gnats, flies, widespread death of livestock, boils, hail and fire, locusts, darkness, and the death of all firstborn people and creatures. So the broader context of Scripture lets us know that the end-time birth pains can come in the form of extreme weather events, mass animal deaths, insect swarms, disease, and other wide-scale calamities.

We clearly see all kinds of extreme convulsions in the natural world today. So much so that even unbelievers notice that the birth pains are getting worse, yet they neglect to acknowledge them as such. Rather, they have attributed these signs to things such as ozone layer depletion, global warming, climate change, and the like—anything but what the Bible tells us they are.

My guess is that as you are reading this lesson, there is a fairly recent plague, epidemic, earthquake, weather-related event, or some other natural disaster that garnered a lot of media attention.

VERSES TO CONSIDER

By the breath of God ice is given, and the broad waters are frozen. Also with moisture He saturates the thick clouds; He scatters His bright clouds. And they swirl about, being turned by His guidance, that they may do whatever He commands them on the face of the whole earth. He causes it to come, whether for correction, or for His land, or for mercy.

—JOB 37:10-14 (NKJV)

We know that the whole creation has been groaning as in the pains of childbirth right up to the present time.

—ROMANS 8:22

There will be great earthquakes, famines and pestilences in various places, and fearful events and great signs from heaven.

—LUKE 21:11

What is the most recent natural catastrophe that has appeared in the news? Have you noticed, in general, an increase in natural disasters over the last few years?

Have you noticed that diseases once thought eradicated are making a comeback, weather events are frequently described as record-breaking, and natural disasters seem to be so much more frequent than they were just 10-20 years ago?

How are the convulsions of nature serving as God's billboard to a watching world?

Even in disaster, God's grace shines through to mankind. Do you agree? Can you think of a specific example or two?

How can we remain hopeful and courageous in the midst of these tumultuous times?

APPLICATION / FURTHER STUDY

It's easy to become fearful these days. Look up the following verses and write down a key phrase from or summary about each.

Isaiah 35:4:

Isaiah 43:1:

Matthew 6:33-34:

John 14:27:

PRAYER

LORD, help me not to fear the convulsions of nature. Help me to remember that you are still the God who calms the seas, answers prayer in the middle of the storm, and sees us through the fire and the flood. If a natural disaster strikes nearby, help me to rise to the occasion by offering hope, courage, help, and prayer to those who need it. When natural disasters strike in areas where I am unable to offer physical help, please remind me to pray and give as you lead. Last, encourage me with the thought that these birth pains are signs of your soon return! In Jesus's name, amen.

Spiritual Signs

(The Non-Prophet's Guide™ to the End Times, Chapter 16)

As mentioned in *The Non-Prophet's Guide™ to the End Times*, there are positive and negative spiritual signs. On the positive side, we are seeing continued explosive growth in the number of conversions to Christianity in areas that are difficult to reach through missionary efforts. We are hearing many reports of significant numbers of people turning to Christ in places like Iran and China. And a growing remnant of believers is awakening to the realization that we are rapidly approaching earth's final moments.

The negative signs continue to escalate as well. Since the writing of *The Non-Prophet's Guide™ to the End Times*, the occult, cults, false teachers, and apostasy in the church have continued to grow unabated.

The net result of the positive and negative spiritual signs is polarization. The "grey area" is fading away and culture is becoming increasingly black and white—good or evil— with very little in between. As we approach the rapture and all that follows, evil is becoming increasingly bold and practiced more and more in the open. This is forcing true believers to either compromise or stand clearly for truth. Light and darkness are becoming more visible in all spheres of influence (politics, entertainment, churches and denominations, etc.).

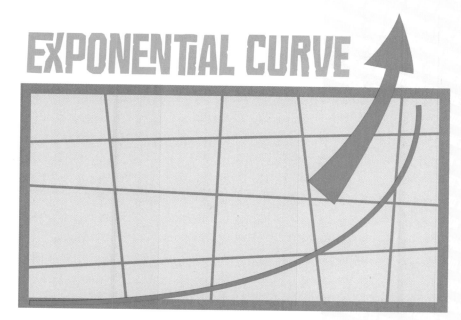

This gospel of the kingdom will be preached in the whole world as a testimony to all nations, and then the end will come.

—MATTHEW 24:14

The Lord is not slow in keeping his promise, as some understand slowness. Instead he is patient with you, not wanting anyone to perish, but everyone to come to repentance.

—2 PETER 3:9

The Spirit clearly says that in later times some will abandon the faith and follow deceiving spirits and things taught by demons.

—1 TIMOTHY 4:1

Nor did they repent of their murders, their magic arts, their sexual immorality or their thefts.

—REVELATION 9:21

STUDY QUESTIONS

Why do you think the gospel needs to go out to the whole world before end-time events unfold?

What does this say about God's patience, grace, and love?

Do you see apostasy getting worse in the church? How so?

How can we distinguish apostates (those who depart from true biblical Christianity) from those who hold to minor errors or who have different convictions about secondary issues?

What are some fundamental tenets of the faith that all believers should hold to?

Do you agree that the persecution of Christians in the West is getting worse? Why or why not?

How can we be more aware of the struggles of the persecuted church of our day?

In what ways have you seen the occult increase its influence upon pop culture, politics, and other arenas of life?

APPLICATION / FURTHER STUDY

Set aside some time to research an aspect of the spiritual signs that you are not familiar with. Suggested topics include persecution, apostasy in the church, Muslims turning to Christianity in large numbers, the explosive growth of the occult in the West, and Jewish people turning to Christ. Make note of ministries and organizations that provide information you can use for your research, and record any statistics or interesting facts that garner your attention.

PRAYER

LORD, there is less and less grey with each passing day. It seems the world is becoming more polarized, and the issues are becoming more black and white. People have become increasingly vocal about choosing evil or righteous causes. Help me to be discerning and to get my cues straight from Scripture and the leading of the Holy Spirit. As the world grows more evil, help me not to fear or give up. Help me to stand and live courageously—and lovingly—in these times in which we live. In Jesus's name, amen.

LESSON 16

SIGNS OF CULTURE

Signs of Culture

(The Non-Prophet's Guide™ to the End Times, Chapter 17)

One of the most telling indicators about the state of culture today is how innocence is treated. Is it protected and maintained, or abused and destroyed? We can get our answer by looking at how people respond to the issue of abortion. In the past, pro-abortion advocates claimed that their desire was for abortion to be safe, legal, and rare. Fast-forward to our day, and that has changed. These advocates no longer attempt to soften the harshness of what they are standing for. They have moved on—to the point that late-term abortion and even out-right infanticide are legal, advocated, and celebrated in some areas of America.

Just a few short years ago gender identity confusion was lovingly treated as a disorder as doctors and parents tried to help children get through a season of perplexity and back to fact-based reality. Now, however, such attempts to offer heartfelt care are rebuffed and children are unquestioningly being given dangerous hormone drugs and pushed into permanently changing their young bodies without careful consideration for scientific and biological realities.

There are many other types of cultural disintegration occurring in our day, but the lack of protection for the innocence and safety of babies and children is one key indicator that this birth pain is increasing in frequency and intensity.

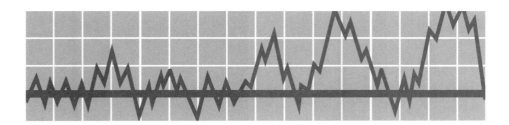

Mark this: There will be terrible times in the last days. People will be lovers of themselves, lovers of money, boastful, proud, abusive, disobedient to their parents, ungrateful, unholy, without love, unforgiving, slanderous, without self-control, brutal, not lovers of the good, treacherous, rash, conceited, lovers of pleasure rather than lovers of God—having a form of godliness but denying its power.

—2 TIMOTHY 3:1-5

Above all, you must understand that in the last days scoffers will come, scoffing and following their own evil desires. They will say, "Where is this 'coming' he promised? Ever since our ancestors died, everything goes on as it has since the beginning of creation." But they deliberately forget that long ago by God's word the heavens came into being and the earth was formed out of water and by water. By these waters also the world of that time was deluged and destroyed.

—2 PETER 3:3-6

STUDY QUESTIONS

What are some examples of delusions or lies that are being infused into culture, politics, and society?

How is this laying the ground for a massive delusion during the tribulation period?

Have you personally encountered scoffers?

Does this type of behavior seem more prevalent today than it was 10 to 20 years ago? Why do you think that is?

The days of Noah and Lot were full of violence and immorality. What parallels do you see between their day and ours?

If you have children or grandchildren, how do you feel about their future right now?

Do you think Western society is currently experiencing the downward spiral described in Romans 1:18-32? Why or why not?

APPLICATION / FURTHER STUDY

Using a computer or smart device, look up one of the major news network sites and briefly skim through the headlines. Now read 2 Timothy 3:1-5. Do you see any of what's happening today described in this passage?

PRAYER

LORD, as the world becomes more lawless, dangerous, and deluded, help me to stay grounded in truth and godly living. Help me, my immediate family, and my extended family to heed your voice and to live godly lives in this dark time. Honestly, Lord, at times it seems impossible to live in this world and not be affected by it. But with you, all things are possible! Help me to be determined to follow you, focus on you, resist the pull of the world, put good people and accountability around me, stay plugged in to a local church body, and apply your Word to my daily walk. I know that I can do all things through Christ, and I pray for your strength to be made perfect in my weakness. In Jesus's name I pray, amen.

LESSON 17

SIGNS OF TECHNOLOGY

LESSON 17

Signs of Technology

(The Non-Prophet's Guide™ to the End Times, Chapter 18)

Daniel 12:4 says that an explosion of knowledge and travel will occur as we approach the end times. I believe the knowledge and "to and fro-ing" is both literal and prophetic in nature. We should expect an era of exponential knowledge growth related to technology and science, and we should expect to see a greater awareness and understanding of the prophecies in Scripture in the time of the end. Similarly, we should expect to see a great increase in travel as well as in people digging deeper into Scripture— going to and fro or cross-referencing passages in the Bible and viewing the patterns of prophetic scripture as a whole.

We do indeed see both layers of this prophecy being fulfilled in our day. It is also significant that the explosion in technology and travel began during the same century that Israel was reborn. This is not mere coincidence. Whether you look at the technology of flight, nuclear power, communications and broadcasting, DNA and microbiology, space exploration, or the Internet, these all materialized during the same century that Israel became a country.

Several prophecies in the Old and New Testaments seem to point to technology that was not available until our generation. Descriptions of what appears to be nuclear explosions, nuclear fallout, global communication and broadcasting, cashless digital systems, missile technology and flight, artificial intelligence, and DNA manipulation can all be found in prophecies related to the end times.

Obviously the terminology used to describe these advances did not exist until our day, but when you carefully study the biblical descriptions and think about how well they fit with certain technologies now available, you can see that our day was foretold in passages that were written 1,900 to 2,600 years ago.

VERSES TO CONSIDER

You, Daniel, shut up the words, and seal the book until the time of the end; many shall run to and fro, and knowledge shall increase.

—DANIEL 12:4 (NKJV)

A.I. and Digital Mark Technology

The second beast was given power to give breath to the image of the first beast, so that the image could speak and cause all who refused to worship the image to be killed.

—REVELATION 13:15

It also forced all people, great and small, rich and poor, free and slave, to receive a mark on their right hands or on their foreheads, so that they could not buy or sell unless they had the mark, which is the name of the beast or the number of its name.

—REVELATION 13:16-17

Nuclear Weapons

A prophecy against Damascus: "See, Damascus will no longer be a city but will become a heap of ruins…In the evening, sudden terror! Before the morning, they are gone!"

—ISAIAH 17:1,14

People will be continually employed in cleansing the land. They will spread out across the land and, along with others, they will bury any bodies that are lying on the ground. After the seven months they will carry out a more detailed search. As they go through the land, anyone who sees a human bone will leave a marker beside it until the gravediggers bury it in the Valley of Hamon Gog, near a town called Hamonah. And so they will cleanse the land.

—EZEKIEL 39:14-16

This is the plague with which the LORD will strike all the nations that fought against Jerusalem: Their flesh will rot while they are still standing on their feet, their eyes will rot in their sockets, and their tongues will rot in their mouths.

—ZECHARIAH 14:12

Broadcasting

For three and a half days some from every people, tribe, language and nation will gaze on their bodies and refuse them burial. The inhabitants of the earth will gloat over them and will celebrate by sending each other gifts, because these two prophets had tormented those who live on the earth.

—REVELATION 11:9-10

STUDY QUESTIONS

How have you seen technology and travel increase during your lifetime?

How have you seen technology being used to spread the gospel?

How can you yourself use technology to spread the gospel and minister to others?

Technology is neutral and can be used for good or evil. In what ways do you see technology being used for good?

In what ways do you see technology being used for evil?

In your own words, how does the development of technology intersect with Bible prophecy?

APPLICATION

To dig deeper, do a quick Internet search to find recent articles about new technological developments. Some areas you could research include chip implant technology and use, satellite-based global Internet, trans-humanism, DNA editing, artificial intelligence, surveillance technology (in China, for example), and military drones. How does your research shed light on various technologies that are necessary for certain end-time events to occur?

PRAYER

LORD, the technology of our day looks more and more like what is described in Revelation and other prophetic passages of Scripture. I am amazed once again at your foreknowledge, and I thank you for sharing this with us in your Word. It seems that only your supernatural restraining power is keeping the world from utter destruction. This too is a fulfillment of prophecy. Help me to understand our times in light of your Word and your purposes. In Jesus's name, amen.

LESSON 18

THE SIGN OF CONVERGENCE

LESSON 18

The Sign of Convergence

(The Non-Prophet's Guide™ to the End Times, Chapter 19)

Longtime prophecy experts, and some who have gone on to be with the Lord, have noted that there used to be very few prophetically significant developments per decade. Then from around the time of Hal Lindsey's book (1971) onward, the number of developments started to increase. Nowadays the number has ramped up dramatically, with noteworthy events occurring with greater frequency!

Even secular futurologists—scientists who study and forecast outcomes based on current data such as population growth, supply and demand, cultural changes, natural resources, and nuclear proliferation—are sounding alarms and saying that exponential curves for various game-changing developments are here or on the very near horizon.

I remember reading the first book in the Left Behind series in 1995, which depicted a future attack on Israel from the north led by Russia, Iran, and Turkey. At the time, this seemed unlikely. The Soviet Union had collapsed in 1991. Turkey had been positioning itself as a Western-friendly country, trying desperately to get into the European Union. In 1990, Syria joined the US-led coalition against Iraq and had been in direct negotiations with Israel. And Israel had to import most of its gas and oil because its massive reserves of both hadn't been discovered yet. So the idea of a Russia-Iran-Turkey alliance didn't seem plausible at the time. Critics mocked those who taught such.

Fast-forward to today. The massive upheaval of the Arab Spring and the resulting civil war in Syria (raging since 2011) quickly led to the coalition of nations mentioned in Ezekiel 38. The US vacated her role as Mideast influencer, opening a vacuum for Russia to move in. Right now, Syria is controlled by Russia, Iran, and Turkey. Those three nations have formal agreements with each other and are attempting to permanently entrench themselves in the country. All three have troops and military equipment throughout Syria. In this way, Iran is forming a land bridge from Tehran to Israel's border. Even the secondary nations mentioned in Ezekiel 38 are aligned. Sudan and Libya are both partnering with one or more of the three main Ezekiel 38 countries. I'm not exaggerating when I write this next statement: The Gog-Magog War could happen at any time. I'm not saying it will, but based on what we see in Ezekiel 38, the stage is set. All that's needed is for a spark to set the fuse.

In addition, all the other end-time signs are in active play right now. Every prophetic indicator is aligning or converging in our day. These are truly exciting times in which to be alive!

VERSES TO CONSIDER

When you see all these things, you know that it is near, right at the door.
—MATTHEW 24:33

When these things begin to take place, stand up and lift up your heads, because your redemption is drawing near.
—LUKE 21:28

What are some ways that end-time conditions have been falling more rapidly into place after Israel's rebirth?

In light of all this, how should we as Christians be living? Put another way, what does it mean to be "more alert"?

Do you think there is any way possible for current conditions to be reversed?

What is the most compelling set of converging signs you see in our day?

How do we know that these prophetic alignments are not just a coincidence? How would you answer someone who thinks they are?

List three to five theological experts whom you highly respect for their knowledge, character, integrity, and faithfulness to God's Word. Take some time to check out their blog posts, podcasts, recent articles, or messages to observe what they are saying about the times in which we live. Make note of anything that gets your attention.

PRAYER

LORD, with the super sign of Israel's rebirth and the increasing and rapid convergence of the other sign categories you instructed us to keep an eye on, it really seems that your return is imminent. I know your desire is that none should perish and that you want as many as possible to become saved before the rapture. With that said, help me to do my part in telling others about the salvation that can be found in Christ alone. I long for your return, Lord. Your bride wants to be with her groom. Even so, come Lord Jesus. Amen.

ENDNOTE

1. Mark Twain, as cited by Tuly Weisz in "Mark Twain's Unwittingly Prophetic Vision for the State of Israel," *Jerusalem Post*, September 23, 2017, https://www.jpost.com/Opinion/Unto-the-nations-505760.

ALSO BY TODD HAMPSON

The Non-Prophet's Guide™ to the End Times

Do you struggle with understanding all the prophecies about the last days? Does it feel like words such as *rapture* and *apocalypse* fly right over your head? You're not alone. It's common to dismiss these and other topics related to Bible prophecy as irrelevant and…well…too complicated.

But *The Non-Prophet's Guide™ to the End Times* changes all that! Prepare to be blessed in an entertaining and meaningful way as this book combines engaging illustrations and down-to-earth explanations to help you navigate the ins and outs of Bible prophecy. There's no better time to grasp God's plan for the future—and for you—than this very moment.

The Non-Prophet's Guide™ to the Book of Revelation

If the final book of the Bible has ever left you scratching your head or wondering what to make of plagues and horsemen, your friendly Non-Prophet is here to help you read Revelation as never before.

Full of fascinating content and graphics, you'll find this a user-friendly guide to the apostle John's prophecies about the last days. This concise and appealing study:

- removes the fear factor and demystifies the capstone book of the Bible
- provides biblical clarity about the key events in the end times
- helps reclaim your hope, confidence, and joy in the promised future

The last days are nearer than ever before. There's no better time to understand the present in light of history's final outcome.